CW00671295

THE MORTAL MAN

Kieron Winn

THE MORTAL MAN

Howtown Press

First published in 2015
by Howtown Press
32 Bridge Street
Oxford OX2 0BA
UK

Reprinted 2015

Printed by Berforts Information Press Ltd, Stevenage

ISBN 978-1-910693-31-5

Acknowledgements

Poems in this collection were published, sometimes in earlier versions, in the following magazines: *Agni*, *Christ Church Matters*, *The Dark Horse*, *The Interpreter's House*, *Literary Imagination*, *The London Magazine*, *The New Criterion*, *New Statesman*, *New Walk*, *Oxford Magazine*, *Plectrum – The Cultural Pick*, *Poetry Review*, *The Spectator*, *The Swansea Review*, *Temenos Academy Review*, *The Times Literary Supplement* and *The Wordsworth Circle.*

Clutag Press printed 'The Gentleman Bowls Along' as a leaflet. Selections of poems appeared in three anthologies: *Oxford Poets 2007* (Carcanet, 2007); *Joining Music with Reason* (Waywiser, 2010); and *Where We Fell to Earth: Writing for Peter Conrad* (privately printed, 2011).

Some of these poems were read during a short film on BBC1, on BBC Radio Kent, and on the American radio station WBUR.

'The Maiden Una' is indebted to the translation of 'The Sought-for Grave' by Barry Jackman in *Twenty Plays of the Nō Theatre*, ed. Donald Keene (Columbia University Press, 1970).

Contents

For Amanda Holton

mine eye has moved o'er three long leagues
Of shining water, gathering, as it seemed,
Through every hair-breadth of that field of light
New pleasure, like a bee among the flowers.

William Wordsworth
The Prelude, Book 1 (1805)

My hands released at last, the cliff soars
Ten thousand metres, the ploughshare sparks,
All's consumed with my body. Born again,
The lanes run straight, the rice well in the ear.

Kanemitsu-Kogun (19th century)
trans. Lucien Stryk and Takashi Ikemoto

THE MORTAL MAN

The Gentleman Bowls Along

For Peter Conrad

The gentleman bowls along, and flourishing his cane
Creates new symbols in the morning air.
His face is sanguine-pink, his waistcoat half unbuttoned;
His liquid eyes reflect stout cattle, orderly hedge;
His brimming heart spills some runaway laughter.
With happiness to hand in breathing, seeing,
Paradise for man cannot be far away.

First Photo

In memory of Jimmy Winn

There I took my first photo: dark-haired, keen,
My father folds my sister in one arm.
He smiles and hears the click of the machine,
The world of oil and men assumed like a blazer,
A blue pullover or a sweet-foiled razor.
Later we visited a cousin's farm
Where one brown room was waxed and Sunday-clean,
But half sunk in the hen yard was a broad
Dull knife whose purpose came and left me awed.

I found his warm, accustomed, skilful hand,
And all was made all right in his broad features,
And everything seemed measured out and planned.
Thirty years later and our fingers tap
As I am passing him a folded map.
I cannot bring a bucket of rock-pool creatures
And have him beam at me and understand,
But it dies hard, wanting someone to say
All will be well, with the power to make it so today.

Over High Street to Patterdale

From the steeple hat of the cairn on Thornthwaite Crag
Dinosaur backs of ridges sloping south
Then mist: drizzling, organic, luminous air;
Hayeswater comes and goes like a lucid thought.
Cold cuts of legs along the Roman road;
Hardy khaki grasses; crouching for cover
By a waterfall in a hollow; then from nowhere
Blue tents by Angle Tarn, and a small shored path
Above the sensuous trench of Patterdale:
Red fern, brown earth, green flanks, aglow like jewels.
Cold lava bears you up as you stride on through
New rain-laid streams that rapidly scan the grit.

Mardale

In 1935 the village of Mardale Green was flooded
to create a reservoir for Manchester.

I

Old lumen-loving lenses make the village
Appear inevitably real and present,
Yet faintly imprecise, as if a spirit
With life and motion. Fells and buildings blend
And seem to make one caramel sweetness, holding
White-fronted mansions, farms with granular walls,
A delta nearly splitting up two lakes
The running beck kept joined, the soft-combed yews
Far taller than the church, and the Dun Bull
(With its own tennis court across the road),
The centre of the famous autumn hunt
When all its sixteen rooms would be snapped up
And other gentlemen would happily sleep
In bathrooms, in the windows, or the stables.

2

Isaac Cookson, forty years a shepherd,
Brings a weak ewe for treatment on the farm.
His features have a steady firecoal valour
And yet, like many natives of the past,
He seems to us a little slow as well,
Antique, with manners weightier than our taste.
Look at the people working on the dam,
Their motorbikes, their level iron-framed houses,
A hungrier kind of life force in their eyes.
The Royal Engineers blew up the farms
With new explosive they were keen to try
And ate beef sandwiches and brewed up tea,
And as the waters rose, the lakes burst open
With eighteen billion rushing precious gallons.

3

When Manchester is thirsty in a drought
People still come to look at Mardale Green,
And stand on Chapel Bridge in red cagoules,
Descendants, in the world of stone and air,
Of long-dead shepherds with their brown pint mugs.
But such a wasting of the fields, the delta,
The delicate twin lakes took place to bring
This summer marvel: ghostly stumps of yews,
And grass regrowing on the tennis court,
And silted dry-stone walls like lengthy bones.
Bluff smiling men unrolling plans might think
A heart that loved the place was bound to find
New comforts, new distractions soon, as though
One farm, one shingly shore is like another.

In the British Museum

The Mausoleum of Halikarnassos

Among colossal rags of statuary,
A hunk of horse, a head, a bride and groom
Whose thighs are gracefully advancing, we
Skitter like hundreds and thousands or packet seeds,
Or tropical fish about a watery tomb.
We pass by captions of heroic deeds,

Borrowing our bright clothes and warm soft skin,
Viewed over skulls and jewels in misting cases.
A Pharaoh's lovely daughter traipses in;
A Roman nose, a clear broad Grecian brow
Are each exhibited in passing faces
Of visitors among the statues now.

In the National Gallery

'Minerva Protects Pax from Mars' by Rubens

A satyr marvels at a cornucopia
As crested fierce Minerva shields pale Pax.
A putto hails this newly-born utopia;
Hymen brings children to the fruitful scene.
The adult figures look both poised and lax.
A nymph, bare-breasted, shakes a tambourine.

I love the trees behind the revelry,
Deciduous, dark-shadowed leaf and bark.
There you can almost see my mother and me,
Ages ago, where Medway waters glide,
Contented with our rounds, our woodland walk,
Ignoring all that strange pomp to the side.

In the National Gallery 2

'View of the Westerkerk, Amsterdam' by van der Heyden

Brick buildings step above the gallant trees
And postered sapling casings. Lovers look
And find each other; someone stops to tease
His motley dog. No waves of tenebrous gloom
Lap around figures from an ancient book.
This world is gleaming, like a scrubbed stone tomb.

To see with such exactness and repose
Is all of prophecy and art in one.
Myths are revealed in dusty humbug clothes,
Working cheap terrors from behind a curtain.
The gravitational and lordly sun
Makes every brick look weighted, placed, and certain.

In the Ashmolean Museum

The Tradescant Collection

Love-shorn, these beached and homeless rarities
Are suffering from a slow delirium:
A swollen shoe that used to pinch or please,
A hazy altar stone of Jupiter's,
A wilted glove, a wizened soundless drum,
Unwhetted swords, and dullened Barbary spurs.

Only this sixteenth-century porcelain,
A wedding ginger jar with shining glaze,
Has something of the watery brightness in
The eyes that danced beside it in Shanghai,
And loved the blooms and dragon it portrays
And found it clean, or brimming, or awry.

In an Oxford Antiquities Shop

Roman oil lamp with erotic scene

Such images left moderns mortified:
A man and woman rear in ecstasy.
This oil lamp was a talking point and guide.
Now blurred by time, near where the flame once played,
The figures keep a kind of privacy,
And grow more universal as they fade,

Showing the dreaming and imagining,
The sameness and distinctiveness of lovers.
Over a thousand pounds for this old thing!
I pass thick colleges while hurrying home,
And find you waiting deep within the covers
Where soon we are rebuilding ancient Rome.

Churches in Rome

For Al and Elisabeth Dutton

Luther was fought with any means: the lour
Of teeming mouldings crowding out delight,
Marble like fatty blood, soft frescoes' blight,
A saint's coarse talons. All this claims the power
To rule and own, to hold the flock in sight,

But these trecento saints have lucent faces.
Awareness decks their bodies like gold leaf.
Christ has an arm around his mother; belief
Is nothing where such kind frank love displaces
Bewildered fear and smart quotidian grief.

Piazza di Spagna, 1860

On the Spanish Steps there sprawls in original sun
Il Padre Eterno with his rusty coat,
His bright paternal pate and hoar-frost beard,
By the fountain modelled on a stranded boat.

It is the lunch break from the studio.
A holy-featured Virgin lies at ease
After a lengthy morning of pietà.
He takes great chunks out of a mighty cheese

And she enjoys a Pantheon-domed loaf.
Both watch amorphous water's fine largesse
Turning to spouts and brilliant shooting drops
Then sinking back to fertile formlessness.

Lost in Rome

We peer at maps below an alien streetlamp.
Outside a box-edged café, heaters blaze.
Almost invisibly, through new piazzas,
We make our way as if through linked-up days.

Alone, I might feel like a ruin lizard
Scuttling beneath a bit of shattered torso,
Or seem no more than transient and jostled
Along the incense-high commercial Corso.

As Rome waves in another January
All feels so gladly willing to be seen,
Like orange trees in wide-surveying gardens,
Casually flaunting jewels among the green.

I never thought I'd have a garden, one
Two of us till and plant, though in a way
Allium, rose and foxglove seem to come
From nowhere. Even in Trastevere

The best of our walled garden and its seeds
Is here, in jokes and eyebeams running true,
Making a force field round us as we go,
And I am never really lost with you.

At the Foot of Gardens

1 Compost

Mounds like low grass huts, they grew at the foot
Of tidy gardens, forkable and moist,
Dilapidated, harmless, almost friendly,
Sweet mulching down of much that had been living,
Hair that mounts up grey on a barber's floor.

2 The Bonfire Before Lighting

Dropleted twigs with the red bloom still on
Jutted out with thorns, made caves within.
A blackbird's corpse, a slow-worm's, all would go.
Dissolution, absolute absence of girders,
Of intellectual property, baroque scales.

3 The Gardener

Gauger of distance in Newtonian worlds,
At home with the cool nails that gleam like fillings,
The creosoted stubble-sheeted shed,
Attics and silences and certain beams
And long snake-patterned straps to hold down luggage,
He sees through all the charlatans and jokers
And never doubts his perfect right to be here.

The Duplicator

My father had a conker-coloured desk,
Buff envelopes, and other jetsam drawn
From London: punch cards, and account-ruled sheets,
And, above all, a useful duplicator
Smelling of ink and spirit. A frail stencil
Was first applied like leaf around the giant
Tarry drum. A handle turned with great
Revolutions of the arm made papers
Airily fall then stack up in the tray.
Orderly duplication of the minutes.
Later, hooded like a hawk, it cooled,
Regained its temper, like a warrior
After a day's work, in a Zen-like calm
Among the ashtrays and the dusty pot plants.

An Old Adventure Show

I loved this programme, and my father drew
Scenes with his hard fine pencil skilfully
To help them last for me. The decades grew
And now I have the show on DVD,

And watch another age, its confidence,
Collars and hems and hair, its sense of splendour
And future times now glossed with innocence,
As infinitely delicate and tender

As the idea of my parents being young,
With their first house, first rose and garden shears,
First caravan, the shades they walked among,
And all they could not know of future years.

Hobbema Print

Beside the wide-eyed, posy-holding children
And the turquoise harbour with its clucking boats,
The Hobbema had power to unsettle.
Among its wooded gloom flared ember-golds

Making a house, uneven as a pile
Of hay bales slyly sinking into themselves.
There were complex trees, and when the hall light
  caught them,
Wild glinting canvas threads. All had its life;

Villagers walked together, deep in secrets.
I sensed the bonds they carried through the dark,
The detail indirect in adult lives.
That painting led into the heart's fierce groves.

Staying with Mabel

In memory of Mabel Westmorland

Reaching into the bag, sand-soft, dark green,
Meant mystery and risk, a clack of runes,
Though no cruel fates were spelt, but word on word
Like *gentle*, *aunt* and *love* in afternoons
When much was scrupulously kept unseen,
Schisms and losses anciently incurred.

Mabel displayed intent subdued prowess,
Mastering wits and chance. Her scores would spell
Roars of delight. She was the centre star
Loud Euston led us to in Motherwell.
Though customs altered, and I saw her less,
Each year she sent the *Scotsman* calendar:

Turning the pages of the last, I see
A summer castle, peaks in fine-sieved snow,
Pristine romantic harbours in the Isles,
Light-casting lochs, and grids of days below
Like frames of film unrolling emptily
Or racks of now unlettered Scrabble tiles.

A British Veteran

A man who held a rifle on the climb
To Passchendaele now bears a bubbling flute.
His hand is strong and rubicund, his frame
Mobile and actual. Watch him turn, salute

Australian great-great-grandsons; woollen cloth
Is covering his body now as then.
That hand will soon slip under the stream of myth.
No one thinks Agincourt was fought by men.

A Photograph Album

They stand with racket or with fishing rod,
With fossil, coin, or other curio,
Each one potentially a household god.
Now they are on the river, now in snow,

Wearing a knitted hat, a patterned scarf,
Amidst the carnage from a snowball fight.
Blurred, here one is caught head back, mid-laugh,
The cause of it forever recondite.

This shows them sitting round a kitchen table,
A gothic radio, and rising up
On shelves, a set of china; we are able
To number every deep capacious cup,

See dragons and pagodas on a plate, a
Swelling teapot. Care, perhaps unspoken,
Preserved it; taken forty-four years later
A picture shows not one piece lost or broken.

Wordsworth and Coleridge

Insufficient, the broad
Oaten flakes,
The convictions plain
As Skiddaw—

How Coleridge would have loved
Neon, glutamates
And so many channels:
Intricate, hare-like, in the end a nuisance.

In Lausanne

I Edward Gibbon

For dry undazzled demolition work,
Mocha is apt. Light skates across the lake

Harrowing old popes from rotten tombs
Where they lay snarling, wound with grisly bands.

Gravity may be balanced in the heavens
With the great liberty of irony,

With confluent glances, or a friend's warm handshake
Earthing the forehead's temples, fraught from labour,

Or the frisson as the daughter of a pastor
Leaves perfume fading in the moted air.

2 T. S. Eliot

The mind that welcomes tributary senses
And leaps beyond its scarf of London smog

Finds itself vanish, and the amplitude
And utter givenness of alp and sight.

Shambling overcoated urban gaits
Are not here, nor a fluey Margate shelter,

Nor testy toppling columns in the bank.
Here even Eliot, repeating *water*,

Found that his mind recovered lake-like stretches
After the torchlight red on sweaty faces.

First Day of Spring in Bath

Quick-flowing creamy light and all cohering:
Faux fanes in gardens, Nash and Wesley's shades,
Gold, gaily weighty houses, rocketing sky
And open hillside turning as I turn,

All witnessed through ancestral engineering,
Small canny bones and inward fine parades
We had no part in, choiceless ear and eye
Meting out pleasure I could never earn.

Walking With You

We have gone down so many oaten roads,
Imperial avenues and wormhole alleys,
Childhood streets like glittering mother lodes,
Mountains mailed in ice and gold-flamed valleys.

To see again that sign before the climb,
The slender pub, the well beside the lake,
Is to step out on every other time
And feel the weaving of the cloth we make.

Today we stumbled through a thicket's shambles,
Snarled in the depredations of the mud,
Lashed at by long and backwards-springing brambles
Marking our flesh with constellated blood,

And it is you wrapped up in bed with me,
Charging on warmth as weariness sublimes,
No space between us, while mercurially
The bell that came from Osney Abbey chimes.

A Believer

He can't tell in from out, and still conflates
Good spirits with good spirits, states with states.

The Maiden Una

After the medieval Noh Play 'The Sought-for Grave'

UNA

Two suitors wrote to me on the same day,
At the same hour, both proclaiming they
Loved me with burning passion. How could I choose
One man, and hurt the man I must refuse?
My parents made that striving pair compete
In tests of skill, but neither could defeat
His rival, for they shared one thread of luck,
And when they tried to strike a mallard duck
Both of their arrows pierced a single wing.
I grieved to see that bird's mate lingering
In reeds near Medley with her broken heart.
Because of me that pair was torn apart
And so, where I had often watched them trawl
The Thames, I drowned myself. Hysterical
With vice-like grief, those men began to crave
Death, and they stabbed each other at my grave.
I am to blame! Centuries pass me by:
I died, and still my terrors do not die.
Each soul, they say, suffers each day the fires
Of eight hundred million four thousand desires
And evil-smelling thoughts. Please set me free.
The world is like a burning house to me.

PRIEST

Your guilt is an illusion! All you need do
Is drop all these obsessions cheating you,
Stuck like a daddy-longlegs in your hair,

Thorns on your dress. Let them go back to nowhere.
Eternal moods have no real power to cling.
Fly from the hell where you are sojourning!

UNA

A chink of brightness shows its acumen!
But no, here come those ghostly appetent men:
My suitors grab my hand and pull me back
And worse a duck, its beak a deadly lack,
Its body steel, has claws that will devour
Me and pluck out my marrow hour by hour.

A Victorian Dreams of Heaven

Let Heaven be a great sweet thaw
Of love gone cold in time or the grave;
The taking of hands
Never thought to be taken again;
The old light in the eyes;

Let Heaven be a great sweet thaw
Of love made numb by jealousy,
Love that dared not act because
Acting would scald and scar like fire.
Let Heaven be an utter release from fear.

July

Ice creams, veranda, sparkling Cornish bay:
Old men look jaunty-classic in the sunlight,
Roman consuls slightly down at heel,
And children swim out to a diving platform
Beyond the boats with names of girls and fays.
On the unwinding vein-like roads, all trammels
Are running out before the sea; in fields
The chlorophyll in salty grass is yielding
Willingly to candescent lifting light.
Elsewhere, the verdant Agincourt discipline
Of men-of-Kent trees, cut out from the pattern,
Long hourless afternoons in pubs on greens;
And on the fellsides, nature at her gaudy,
Old catholic colours in the sky and thorn,
Lake like a blue giant tough-skinned basking lizard,
All colours thick as in a childhood film stock.
In Oxford, students sleek with many an A
Dawdle down the river, playing their part,
And languid fellows decorate the meadows;
Imperial ironies are cultivated
In their straw hats and floppy creasing suits.
Summer professional yet legendary:
Great banner in the heavens, read by all.

In the Garden

Neptune, open-mouthed, discredited,
Spouts from the fountain on our rosy wall.
This August evening air is equable.
I fetch a bottle from our earthy shed
By swags of grapes that hang in green and red,
And from our complex wrought-iron chairs we call
The talkative cat, watch campanile-tall
Hollyhocks nodding to us from their bed
Then pick some berries. How can I begin
To thank you for all you give and understand?
Icebergs have shrunk to icecubes, topped with gin.
House martins sew the sky. A bumblebee
Goes stumbling round the blue hibiscus tree,
Coated in pollen like a boy in sand.

T. S. Eliot in Bermuda

Swimming, as ever, helps with all my ailments.
My tender wife is singing in the bedroom.

I have become a classic. I look at my book
And contemplate changing the species of a crab.

The spirit sleeps in such places. Let me enjoy
My yellow silk pyjamas, I am no Dante.

My heart is going: I would enjoy some sherbet.
Later today we may go out to buy some.

In this afterlife, I need not exert myself.
Now I have done my work. I whistle and live.

Heaney's First Collaboration with Eminem

Or, From Digging Potatoes to Digging Swedes

Or, A Bog-Standard Rap

'There is this guy Eminem.
He has created a sense of what is possible.' Seamus Heaney

I was born at the family stack down at Mossbawn
And my legs went to frogspawn (as I later told Hobsbaum)
When I saw a real phat frog (you listening dog?),
Ran off like a girl and fell in a bog,
Met a man from Grauballe who'd pissed his tribe off
And brought back the springtime allegedly (cough).
When I was young I was all earth and fire
(I once missed a comet! Man, I musta been wired)
But then I got down with light and water and brim
And writing my new bag, pantheist hymns,
And the lupins keep growing in my back yard
And my hair's like a cloud and I don't talk too loud,
And the wolves came down on the fucking fold
Like benevolent Swedes, and all's right with the world.

The Later Wordsworth

As coffins pause upon the resting stone,
Rydal Water looks, in human age,
Farther and sweeter, moral and sororal,
Hardening to a darkly-limned engraving,
Or early photograph, profoundly still.

By the old church the beck is quick as ever.
Is there a way back to the spring of life,
A sweetness running in all living blood,
When eyes can see beyond their palimpsest,
Costing the grip on silver, title, cellar?

The Silver Birch

The silver birch against heraldic sky
Is all-consuming: what I am walking through
Is both my garden on a crisp March morning
Under this bounding, binding, human blue,

And a mind cleared of its old reports and annuals.
All that I see is live. I gaze and gaze.
This is full screen in brilliant definition.
I could be rapt at winter's greyest greys.

St Ives

Ash and dust were blown from me by those
Vast and simple packs and bands of colour:
Nutritious, licorous, mackerel-tinted waves,
A solid lapis sky, and platinum sand
That made a massy drawstring purse in the palm.
Dashing and surfing rays were missing nothing,
Lighting every door and stone and corner
To plain and storybook equality,
And mildness I remember as a child,
A nobody, before such adult forces.

Ambleside to Glenridding

Climb on a pony track past meteorite-grottoes
To High Sweden Bridge, a lone constructed eye,
A glimpse of civilization, then press on
To a prehuman valley in the mountains,
Networked by veins of thin and plashable streams.
Now up, an easy up, with Fairfield left,
Mist and moisture cool on grateful limb,
Loved wideness, thereness, love like sun on stone,
To a broken ridge, the start of dirty walking,
Oikish grass and ankle-killing holes,
But there is light and we have time and food;
So Brothers Water inches round a hill,
Lake like a flat grey pebble, and reaching earth
We head past waterfall and fiery fern,
Past Goldrill to the silver spill of Ullswater,
Its miles of absolute edge as mild as Jesus,
Then to the Travellers Rest for woods-floor beer,
Rich seasoned beef, potatoes piping, whisky
And shortbread, fire and sugar for the next day.